THE MOCKTAIL MANUAL

OVER 90 DELICIOUS NON-ALCOHOLIC DRINKS | FERN GREEN

THE MOCKTAIL MANUAL

OVER 90 DELICIOUS NON-ALCOHOLIC DRINKS

FERN GREEN

hardie grant books

CONTENTS

INTRODUCTION

The Mocktail Manual is the book that answers all those no-booze needs. From shakes that offer flavoured creams to die for to jugs of delight and colour, dream mocktails and seasonal delights; this compendium of delectable thirst quenchers will give you the edge when it comes to mixing an exciting non-alcoholic drink.

Making a good drink from scratch can sometimes be hard; knowing where to start is key. Do you want something fizzy, juicy or smooth? Flick through this selection at your own pace and discover the array of delicious flavours you can make. As well as mixing up your drink of choice, why not add an interesting syrup or fruit-popping ice cube to bring it to the next level (see pages 26–31).

So whether you're trying to detox, lose weight, are designated driver, pregnant or just fancy a deliciously refreshing drink, this is the manual to show you how to do it.

Part One:
THE SET-UP

1. EQUIPMENT
2. GLASSWARE
3. STORE CUPBOARD
4. SYRUPS
5. FLAVOURED ICE CUBES

1

EQUIPMENT

Keep it simple is the motto. Even with this marvellous selection of drinks, which involve being muddled, whizzed, stirred and steeped, you will be surprised at how little apparatus is needed. Take a look at these handy tools and see how many you own already!

⊕ COCKTAIL SHAKER OR MASON JAR

To meld all the flavours and cool the drink at the same time, you need a vessel to shake your mix in. The cocktail shaker is the traditional hand blender that makes you look like you know what you are doing. Plus it's easy to use: pour in the liquid, add ice, close the top and away you go. However, if you don't have one of these and are less worried about style, try a Mason jar or large jam jar. Both of these make it still possible to shake vigorously, and you can even see through the glass to watch your drink blend together.

⊕ BOSTON GLASS OR PINT GLASS

When you are making a long drink and need some extra volume in your cocktail shaker, use a Boston glass which comes with the shaker – it is the best way to blend. Alternatively, you can also use an ordinary pint glass with a shaker; this works just as well.

⊙ THE BLENDER

This essential tool makes your life easier on many levels. From making smoothies to shakes, blending fruit into an intense pulp is sometimes what you need to extract all that flavour. All done with the flick of a switch, the more powerful machines are the best – those that can crush ice are even better.

⊙ HAWTHORN STRAINER OR TEA STRAINER

To get that clean, smooth finish on your drink, you may need to strain it. The posh hawthorn strainer fills you with confidence and makes you look like a pro, but a tea strainer can also do the job.

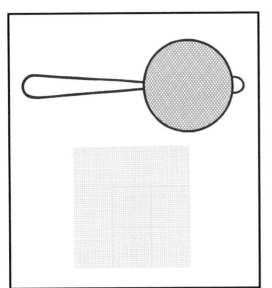

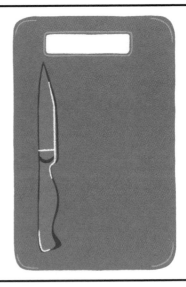

⚙ SIEVE AND MUSLIN

These are both used for taking out those naughty pips and excluding bits when you don't think they are appropriate. Handy for making larger drink quantities for a crowd.

⚙ CHOPPING BOARD AND KNIFE

A board solely used for preparing fresh fruit and veg can be helpful to keep to one side. Chopping up a strawberry where you have had last night's garlic can taint the overall flavour somewhat, so be careful! Knives are your friend – look after them – a handy serrated knife for thick-skinned fruit or a simple paring knife are useful.

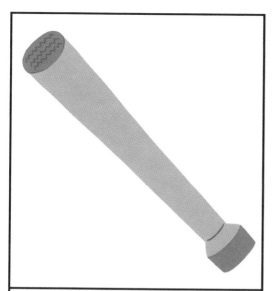

⬆ MUDDLER OR ROLLING PIN

This wooden tool is great at mushing, bashing and bruising up the fruit needed in mocktails and seasonal drinks. It also helps to extract the oils out of lovely fresh herbs. If you are in need of a home-made muddler, try the end of a rolling pin.

JUG

Necessary large container for those very long shared drinks, like punches, fruity waters and shakes. Useful for steeping liquids, leaving them overnight in the fridge. Plus it helps you pour the drink more successfully into the glass for its final descent.

VEGETABLE PEELER

These wide peelers are essential for making those long wide ribbons of cucumber or funky citrus peel, among other glass decor.

MICROPLANE OR FINE GRATER

For the much-needed flavour-enhancing boost of citrus fruits, the Microplane is a handy tool to use. The bog-standard grater does this job pretty well too.

WOODEN SPOON

Classic item found in every kitchen drawer or utensil jar – great for stirring drinks in large jugs.

TABLESPOON AND TEASPOON

These measures are usually helpful for cooking, but some drink recipes only need a particularly small amount of an ingredient, which could swing the taste either way.

GLASSWARE

The vessel used to hold your drink can sometimes be as important as the liquid itself. Glasses come in all shapes and sizes, and here are just a few standard ones that will work well for the drinks in this book. Make sure you keep them clean and sparkly!

⊙ THE CUP OR MUG

Hot drinks need a sturdier container and china or glass is appropriate. Cups are popular for tea but a mug has a more comforting style, which can bring out the best in a hot chocolate.

⊙ THE SLIM JIM OR TALL GLASS

Slender and smart, and ideal for an ice cube or two. Happily takes an adventurous garnish due to its small circumference.

⬆ THE CHAMPAGNE FLUTE

Smart and sophisticated, it usually comes out for a celebration.

⬅ THE HIGHBALL OR PINT GLASS

This large vessel can be used for those long drinks. It is wider than the Slim Jim, is usually filled with ice and often comes with a straw.

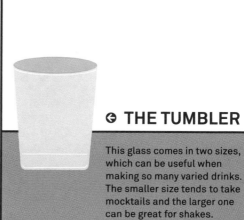

⬅ THE TUMBLER

This glass comes in two sizes, which can be useful when making so many varied drinks. The smaller size tends to take mocktails and the larger one can be great for shakes.

STORE
CUPBOARD

Flavour enhancers to boost your drinks in a variety of ways. The store cupboard can also extend to your kitchen windowsill or garden if you are partial to growing a few herbs – essential to many recipes here.

HONEY, AGAVE NECTAR OR DATES

These are life's great natural sweeteners, taking the sharpness or sourness out of your drink. Squirted, spooned on or de-stoned, these ingredients can be helpful in many ways.

GOLDEN GRANULATED SUGAR

Unrefined sugar that has not been overprocessed. Brings a richer flavour that enhances the drink and gives your syrups a golden tinge and a real edge.

COCOA POWDER

Dried, roasted cocoa beans that have been ground into powder after the cocoa butter has been removed. An essential ingredient for making drinks taste chocolatey.

HERBS

Mint, rosemary, lavender, thyme and basil – all these lovely flavours are great in fresh-tasting fruity waters and muddled with other ingredients to make mouth-watering mocktails. Try making your own tea blend with your favourite herbs – they taste so much better using fresh herbs! Plus, growing them yourself is therapeutic and rewarding.

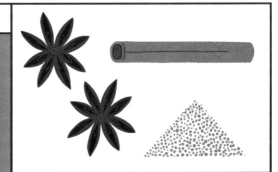

DAIRY

Yoghurts, milks and ice cream. These should be stored in your fridge or freezer, not your store cupboard, and are three common items for your weekly shop. They can help bring creaminess and thickness to a shake or a smoothie, making the drink roll over the tongue like velvet.

SPICES

Star anise has a great flavour and can perk up a drink no end. Cayenne pepper, coriander, cinnamon and nutmeg are all useful spices that can give a simple drink a complex flavour and turn it into something quite unique.

SYRUPS

These lovely sugary gems are great to add into drinks to enhance their flavour and give them an edge. Play with your own flavour combinations by starting with a simple syrup, then explore the heights and depths of different ingredients to pack a punch.

Granulated sugar is used as it brings a richer flavour to the syrup, but feel free to experiment with darker sugars to build up the richness. You can also use these syrups to drizzle over cakes, meringues and ice creams.

SIMPLE SUGAR SYRUP

Ingredients
350 g (12 oz/scant 1⅔ cups)
 granulated sugar
700 ml (24 oz) water

Equipment
saucepan
wooden spoon
jug or bowl and funnel
lidded glass jars or bottles,
 sterilised

Method
Place the sugar and water in a saucepan over a low heat. Slowly bring the mixture up to a simmer and continue to simmer, stirring occasionally, until all the sugar has dissolved. Pour the syrup into the jars or bottles and add the lids. This can keep for up to 1 month in the fridge.

HONEY LAVENDER SYRUP

Ingredients
500 ml (17 oz) water
480 ml (16 oz) honey
4 tablespoons fresh lavender
 buds

Equipment
lidded saucepan
wooden spoon
sieve lined with muslin
jug or bowl and funnel
lidded glass jars or bottles,
 sterilised

Method
Place the water and honey in a saucepan over a low heat and slowly bring up to a simmer. When the honey has dissolved stir in the lavender, remove from the heat, cover and leave to steep for 6–8 hours. Strain the syrup through the lined sieve into a large jug or bowl, then transfer it into the jars or bottles. Put the lids on the containers and store in the fridge for up to 1 month.

GINGER AND PEAR SYRUP

Ingredients
375 ml (12½ oz) water
300 g (10½ oz/scant 3¼ cups)
 granulated sugar, plus
 1 tablespoon
2 ripe pears, peeled,
 cored and chopped
2 tablespoons fresh ginger,
 chopped
1 cinnamon stick

Equipment
lidded saucepan
wooden spoon
sieve lined with muslin
jug or bowl and funnel
lidded glass jars or bottles,
 sterilised

Method
Place the water in the saucepan and add 1 tablespoon of sugar along with the pears and ginger. Slowly bring up to a boil over a medium heat and simmer for 5 minutes. Add the rest of the sugar and cinnmamon and bring the liquid up to the boil, then turn down the heat and simmer, stirring occasionally, until all of the sugar has dissolved. Remove from the heat, cover and leave to steep for 6–8 hours. Strain the syrup through the lined sieve into a jug or large bowl, then pour into jars or bottles. Add the lids to the containers and store in the fridge for up to 1 month.

SWEET ROSE SYRUP

Ingredients
350 ml (12 oz) water
350 g (12 oz/scant 3¼ cups)
 granulated sugar
petals from 6 large (damask)
 roses, gently massaged and torn
 (use pesticide-free roses)

Equipment
lidded saucepan
wooden spoon
sieve lined with muslin
jug or bowl and funnel
lidded glass jars or bottles,
 sterilised

Method
Place the water and sugar in the saucepan over a medium heat and bring to the boil. Turn down the heat and simmer, stirring occasionally, until all the sugar has dissolved. Remove from the heat, stir in the rose petals, cover and steep for 7–8 hours. Strain the syrup through the lined sieve into a jug or bowl, then pour it into the jars or bottles. Put on the lids and store in the fridge for up to 1 month.

Alternatively you could make this syrup with rosewater: Use 300 ml (10 oz) water to 300g (10 oz) sugar to 1–3 drops of rosewater. No need to sieve; just let it cool after boiling and then pour into your jar or container.

LEMON AND GINGER SYRUP

Ingredients
300 ml (10 oz) water
300 g (10 oz/scant 3¼ cups)
 granulated sugar
50 g (2 oz) ginger, peeled and
 finely chopped
300 ml (10 oz) freshly squeezed
 lemon juice

Equipment
saucepan
wooden spoon
sieve lined with muslin
jug or bowl and funnel
lidded glass jars or bottles,
 sterilised

Method
Pour the water into the saucepan, then add the sugar and ginger. Bring the mixture up to the boil, then reduce the heat and simmer, stirring occasionally, until all the sugar has dissolved. Remove the pan from the heat, stir in the lemon juice and strain the syrup through the lined sieve into a jug or bowl and leave to cool. Pour into the jars or bottles, put on their lids and then keep in the fridge for up to 1 month.

ALMOND SYRUP

Ingredients
550 ml (18½ oz) water
275 g (10 oz/2⅔ cups) ground
 almonds
675 g (1 lb 8 oz/generous 3 cups)
 granulated sugar
1½ tablespoons almond extract
juice of 1 orange

Equipment
saucepan
wooden spoon
sieve lined with muslin
jug or bowl and funnel
lidded glass jars or bottles,
 sterilised

Method
In a saucepan over a high heat, bring the water to the boil. Stir in the almonds and bring the mixture back up to the boil. Remove the pan from the heat and set aside to cool. Strain the liquid through the lined sieve into a jug or bowl, then return the liquid to the pan. Add the sugar, almond extract and orange juice, then bring the mixture to the boil. Reduce the heat and simmer, stirring occasionally, until all the sugar has dissolved. Remove from the heat and allow to cool. Pour into jars or bottles. Put the lids on the containers and keep in the fridge to up to 1 month.

FLAVOURED
ICE CUBES

Flavoured ice cubes are a great idea if you want to freeze more flavour into your drinks; no one's a fan of watered-down beverages. These ice cubes look rather impressive floating in a glass too. Go to town with ideas of what to freeze, from tomato juice to orange peel, but make sure the idea makes sense with the refreshment of choice.

WHAT YOU NEED:

Ice cube trays and space in your freezer where you can lay the trays down flat.

HOW TO DO IT:

Choose the liquid and, if using, ingredient(s) – such as pieces of fruit – that you want to make ice cubes with. If you are including ingredients, put small pieces of them into each hole of the ice cube tray first. Pour the liquid into the tray, then freeze for at least 4 hours or until frozen solid.

Here are some examples to start with... ➲

⬆ LEMON OR LIME

The trick here is to cut your lemon or lime segments into small neat pieces so that they fit well in your ice cube tray. Try cutting them into small triangles with the skin on, to add some colour. Use either water or, for a really powerful flavour, the juice from the fruits to freeze the segments in.

Mint and basil leaves look great in ice cubes, and give them a sophisticated air. Use small leaves and fill the trays up with coconut water, sparkling or tonic water or depending on what goes best with the drink they will be going into.

⬆ HERBS

⬆ FRUIT

A raspberry or half a strawberry look really special when frozen in time. Frozen grapes or large cubes of watermelon are perfect for using as ice cubes as they are (with no added liquid). Have a play with all kinds of fruit, from berries to bananas. You will have so much fun you might find the freezer isn't big enough!

If you are having an iced tea or coffee on a boiling hot day, why not top it off with some frozen tea or coffee cubes? Using ice cubes made from brewed tea or coffee stops the drink tasting watered down as they melt, and makes it last much longer – it's win-win!

⬇ TEA OR COFFEE

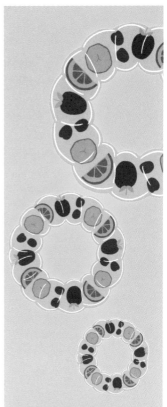

⬆ ICE RING

To make an ice ring for a punch bowl, fill a Bundt tin or a tube pan with water or fruit juice and slices of fruit. Freeze for several hours. Turn out when you need it.

Part Two: THE MOCKTAIL LIST

TEAS

Hot or iced, tea is an essential drink which we'd all like to learn to master. How long do you steep your bag for? Try making these brews using fresh herbs and spices and mix it up a bit. You can also add ice and fruit like our southern European friends.

SPEARMINT TEA

❶ INGREDIENTS

750 ML (25 OZ) WATER
HANDFUL OF SPEARMINT LEAVES (FRESH OR DRIED)
SUGAR OR HONEY, TO TASTE (OPTIONAL)

❷ EQUIPMENT

KETTLE   SAUCEPAN   JUG   SIEVE   TEACUP

❸ METHOD

Boil the water in the kettle. Add the mint to a saucepan and pour over the boiling water. Simmer over a low heat for about 10 minutes. Strain the tea into a large jug and stir in some sugar or honey to taste, if you like, before serving in teacups.

SERVES 2

Green-fingered types like this tea, as they can grow a spearmint shrub in the garden. What could be easier than picking a few sprigs after supper every night to settle the old stomach?

GINGER, LIME & HONEY TEA

❶ INGREDIENTS

750 ML (25 OZ) WATER • 1 LIME, SLICED
5 CM (2 IN) PIECE GINGER, CUT INTO
APPROX. 5 MM (¼ IN) THICK ROUNDS
1 TABLESPOON HONEY

❷ EQUIPMENT

KETTLE   SAUCEPAN   JUG   SIEVE   WOODEN   TEACUP
                                   SPOON

❸ METHOD

SERVES 2
Some like it more limey, others more
gingery, so feel free to tweak the
quantities to suit your taste.

Boil the water in the kettle. Add the lime
and ginger to a saucepan and pour over the
boiling water. Simmer over a low heat for
about 10 minutes. Stir in the honey.
Pour through a strainer or sieve into a jug
and serve immediately.

CHAI TEA

❶ INGREDIENTS

5 CM (2 IN) PIECE GINGER, GRATED • 3 CARDAMOM PODS, SEEDS ONLY • 500 ML (17 OZ) MILK
3 TABLESPOONS SUGAR • 3 TABLESPOONS CHAI TEA LEAVES • GROUND CINNAMON, TO SERVE

❷ EQUIPMENT

SAUCEPAN   JUG   SIEVE   WOODEN SPOON   TEACUP

❸ METHOD

Put the ginger, cardamom seeds, milk and sugar into a saucepan and bring to the boil. Turn the heat down and simmer for 20 minutes. Stir in the tea leaves and continue to simmer for another 5 minutes. Strain the tea into a jug then serve in teacups with a sprinkling of ground cinnamon on top.

SERVES 2
Delicious Indian spiced milky tea that comforts and heals as you sip.

PEACH ICED WHITE TEA

1.5 LITRES (3 PINTS 3 OZ) WATER • 5 WHITE TEA BAGS
4 TABLESPOONS BROWN SUGAR • 2 PEACHES, PITTED
AND DICED • ICE CUBES, TO SERVE

❷ EQUIPMENT

SAUCEPAN | 2 MIXING BOWLS | JUG | SIEVE | WOODEN SPOON | TEACUP

❸ METHOD

Boil the water, remove from the heat and add
the tea bags and 3 tablespoons sugar. Steep
for 5 minutes. Pour the tea minus the bags
into a large bowl and cool for 45 minutes. Add
the remaining sugar to the peaches and let
it sit for 5 minutes to soften before adding to
the jug (no straining). Pour over the cooled
tea, stir and chill. Serve with ice cubes.

SERVES 4
Very popular in Europe, where it is sold in
a bottle or can and pumped with sugar.
This version, on the other hand, has only a
fraction of the sugar and tastes amazingly
fresh – perfect for a summer's day.

EARL GREY WITH ORANGE PEEL

This black tea contains a little oil extracted from the rind of a bergamot orange. By adding some more orange peel you really enhance this flavour and bring it up to new heights.

SERVES 4

❶ INGREDIENTS

1 litre (34 oz) water

4 tablespoons Earl Grey tea leaves, or 12 teabags

peel of 1 orange

1 orange, sliced, to serve

❷ EQUIPMENT kettle, vegetable peeler, saucepan, sieve, jug, 4 small teacups

❸ METHOD
Boil the water in the kettle. Add the tea leaves or bags to a saucepan along with the orange peel. Pour over the boiling water and let it steep for around 5 minutes. Strain the tea into a jug and discard the tea leaves or bags and the orange peel. Pour the tea back into the saucepan and reheat it to your preferred temperature before serving with slices of orange.

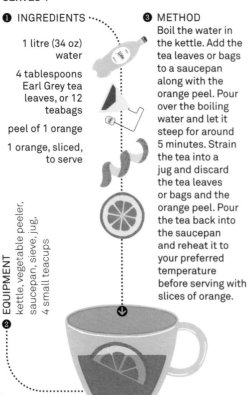

MORNING TEA

Imagine if all your herbal teabags had disappeared from your cupboard. Well, here is one you can make yourself.

SERVES 2

❶ INGREDIENTS

750 ml (25 oz) water

4 lemongrass sticks, bashed

handful of dried lemon verbena leaves

1 liquorice root, bashed

5 cm (2 in) piece ginger, sliced into rounds

❷ EQUIPMENT kettle, saucepan, sieve, jug, 2 small teacups

❸ METHOD
Boil the water in a kettle. Add the lemongrass, dried verbena, liquorice and ginger to a saucepan and pour over the boiling water. Simmer over a low heat for 20 minutes. Strain into a jug and serve immediately.

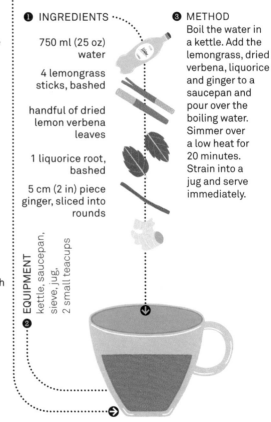

LEMON VERBENA TEA

'Lemony snickets!' is what you could say if you have a cup of this!

SERVES 2

① INGREDIENTS

750 ml (25 oz) water

2 handfuls of dried lemon verbena leaves

honey, to taste (optional)

② EQUIPMENT
kettle, lidded saucepan, sieve, jug, 2 small teacups

③ METHOD
Boil the water in a kettle. Add the lemon verbena to a saucepan and pour over the boiling water. Cover the pan and leave to steep for 5 minutes. Strain the tea into a jug and serve immediately. Add some honey to taste, if you like.

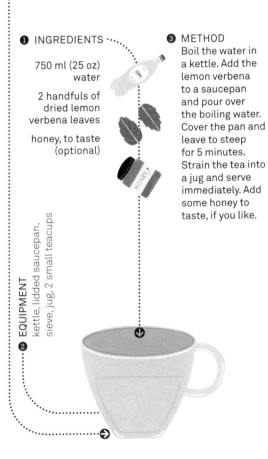

SWEET STRAWBERRY ICED TEA

Jam-packed with strawberries and deliciously refreshing. Try serving with strawberry ice cubes added to the glass before pouring over the tea.

SERVES 4

① INGREDIENTS

1.5 litres (2½ pints) water

5 English breakfast teabags

125 g (4 oz) sugar

500 g (1 lb 2 oz) ripe strawberries

juice of 1 lemon

strawberry ice cubes (see pages 30–31), to serve (optional)

② EQUIPMENT
saucepan, wooden spoon, blender, sieve, jug, 4 small teacups

③ METHOD
Boil the water in a saucepan. Remove from the heat, add teabags. Steep for 5 minutes. Remove the teabags, stir in the sugar, and leave to cool. Purée the strawberries then pass them through a sieve into a jug, and add the lemon juice. Pour the cooled tea into the jug and chill in the fridge. Serve with strawberry ice cubes if you like.

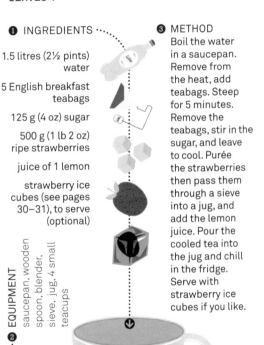

SMOOTHIES

Your fruit bowl is overloaded, or that peach tree in the garden is heavily laden. Or perhaps you have too many strawberries to know what to do with. Well, here are several ideas to start you off – smoothies that you can jam-pack with fruit, add a little yoghurt or juice to and even some veg, then chuck in a blender and away you go. Make them for breakfast, satisfy your fruit craving in the afternoon or simply make one off the cuff as and when you fancy.

BLUEBERRYLICIOUS

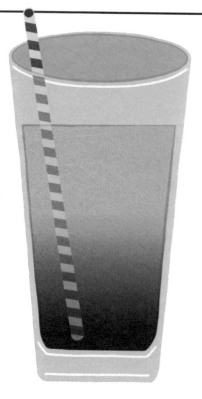

❶ INGREDIENTS

1 BANANA, PEELED • 225 G (8 OZ) FRESH OR FROZEN BLUEBERRIES • 125 G (4 OZ) ALMOND BUTTER 120 ML (4 OZ) ALMOND MILK • 3 DATES, PITTED AND CHOPPED • 200 ML (7 OZ) WATER

❷ EQUIPMENT

BLENDER   TALL GLASS

❸ METHOD

SERVES 1
Plumped up balls of blue whizzed up with a hint of sweet almond.

Put all the ingredients into a blender and whizz until smooth. Serve in a tall glass with a straw.

GREEN SMOOTHIE

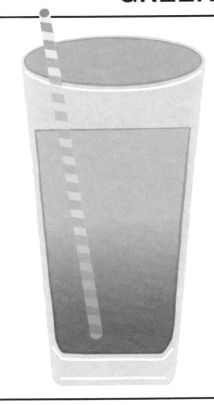

❶ INGREDIENTS

2 HANDFULS OF ROUGHLY CHOPPED KALE
JUICE OF 1 LIME • ½ CUCUMBER, CHOPPED
2 APPLES, CORED AND CHOPPED • 1 AVOCADO,
DE-STONED AND SKIN REMOVED
200 ML (7 OZ) WATER

❷ EQUIPMENT

BLENDER   TALL GLASS

SERVES 1

Avocado is a great ingredient for any smoothie, as it adds creaminess as well as goodness. Chuck in a load of other goodies and you have yourself the king of green smoothies.

❸ METHOD

Add all the ingredients to a blender and blitz until smooth. If you find the consistency a bit thick, add a little more water and blend again. Serve in a tall glass with a straw.

BREAKFAST SMOOTHIE

No time to grab a bowl of porridge? Here is the solution: a breakfast smoothie made the night before. With added bee pollen to give you that boost of energy, stick a straw in it and away you go.

SERVES 2

❶ INGREDIENTS

90 g (3¼ oz) rolled oats

300 ml (10 oz) almond milk

300 ml (10 oz) buttermilk

1 teaspoon bee pollen

2 bananas, peeled

2 tablespoons honey

❷ EQUIPMENT mixing bowl, blender, 2 large glasses

❸ METHOD
Soak the oats in the almond milk in a bowl for 5 minutes. Tip the mixture into a blender along with the remaining ingredients and whizz until smooth. Add a little water and blend again if the consistency is too thick. Pour into large glasses and serve with straws.

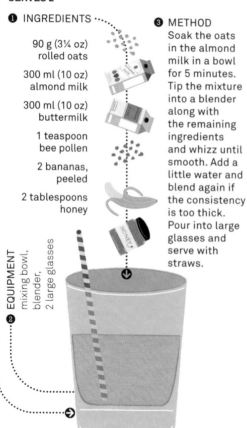

BERRY NANA SMOOTHIE

Strawberries and bananas taste like they always should be together. You can't go wrong with this.

SERVES 1

❶ INGREDIENTS

2 bananas, peeled

12 strawberries, hulled

200 ml (7 oz) natural yoghurt

4 ice cubes

❷ EQUIPMENT blender, tall glass

❸ METHOD
Add all the ingredients into a blender and whizz until smooth. If you feel the consistency is too thick just add a little bit of water. Serve in a tall glass with a straw.

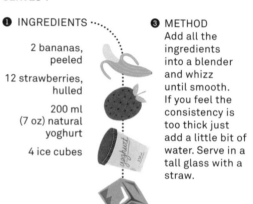
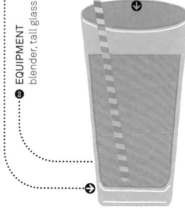

MANGO & RASPBERRY SMOOTHIE

Beautifully pink with big mango sweetness against small raspberry tartness – a mouthful of sunshine!

SERVES 1

1 INGREDIENTS

250 g (9 oz) fresh or frozen raspberries

150 ml (5 oz) whole milk

1 ripe mango, peeled and chopped

150 ml (5 oz) orange juice

3 METHOD
Blitz all the ingredients together in a blender until smooth. If you wish, you can pass the smoothie through a sieve into a jug to remove the raspberry seeds, or you can just drink it as is. Pour into a large tumbler and serve with a straw.

2 EQUIPMENT
blender, sieve (optional), jug (optional), large tumbler

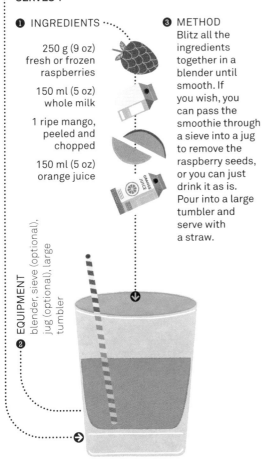

CHOCOLATE & NUT SMOOTHIE

The nuttiness of peanut butter is really tasty in a smoothie. It adds a bit of saltiness to the sweetness of the banana and chocolate... better than a chocolate bar.

SERVES 1

1 INGREDIENTS

1 banana, peeled

2 teaspoons cocoa powder

2 tablespoons peanut butter

300 ml (10 oz) coconut milk

1 teaspoon honey (optional)

3 METHOD
Put all of the ingredients into a blender and blitz until smooth; you can add in or omit the honey depending on how sweet you like your smoothie. If the consistency is too thick, just add a little water. Pour into a large tumbler and serve with a straw.

2 EQUIPMENT
blender, large tumbler

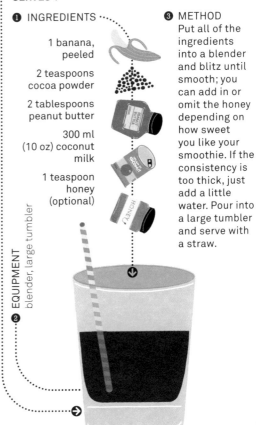

47

PINEAPPLE & COCONUT SMOOTHIE

With the sweetness of fresh pineapple and the creaminess of coconut, you can't go wrong with this tropical island-style smoothie.

SERVES 2

Ingredients
½ ripe pineapple, skin removed and chopped, plus extra to serve
1 banana, peeled
300 ml (10 oz) vanilla yoghurt
300 ml (10 oz) coconut milk
4 ice cubes, to serve

Equipment
blender, 2 tall glasses

Method
Put all of the ingredients except the ice cubes together in a blender and whizz until smooth. Slice 2 triangles of pineapple and make a cut halfway through each piece so they can perch at the top of each glass. Add ice to the tall glasses, pour over the smoothie, garnish with a piece of pineapple and serve with straws.

GOOD MORNING COFFEE SMOOTHIE

If you are into iced coffee, then this takes it one step further. This smoothie not only gives you that hit of coffee, but it fills you up with banana and dates to keep you going a bit longer.

SERVES 2

Ingredients
225 ml (8 oz/1 cup) strong brewed coffee
1 banana, peeled
200 ml (7 oz) natural yoghurt
2 dates, pitted and halved
1 teaspoon ground cinnamon
4 ice cubes

Equipment
blender, 2 tall glasses

Method
Put all of the ingredients into a blender and blend until smooth. Serve in tall glasses.

DETOX SMOOTHIE

If you want to give your body a boost, cleanse the soul and feel good about yourself, then this is the smoothie for you! Packed full of greens and a few alkalisers, this smoothie should help to keep you away from the doctor.

SERVES 2

Ingredients
1 handful of chopped kale
1 handful of spinach
1 banana, peeled
2 apples, cored and chopped
small handful of seedless grapes
juice of 1 lime
600 ml (20 oz) water

Equipment
blender, 2 tall glasses

Method
Whizz all of the ingredients together in a blender until smooth. Serve in tall glasses with straws.

SWEET POTATO & YOGHURT SMOOTHIE

This creamy root vegetable adds a fantastic colour and a spicy and comforting flavour.

SERVES 2

Ingredients
3 small sweet potatoes, peeled and chopped
250 ml (8½ oz) water
375 ml (12½ oz) almond milk
2 teaspoons vanilla extract
3 dates, pitted and halved
1 teaspoon ground cinnamon
½ teaspoon of ground nutmeg
½ teaspoon ground cardamom
120 ml (4 oz) vanilla yoghurt

Equipment
saucepan, colander, blender, 2 tall glasses

Method
Bring a saucepan of water to the boil, add the sweet potatoes and simmer until tender. Drain and set aside. Transfer the cooled potatoes to a blender with the remaining ingredients. Whizz with a little water until smooth. Pour into tall glasses and serve with straws.

MOCKTAILS

There is no mocking these fun, refreshing and sometimes fizzy drinks. Perfect for any party setting, celebration or to get you in the mood for an evening out. This selection of bar scene drinks, from a Pussyfoot (see page 53) to a Blondie (see page 58), abstain from alcohol but do not scrimp on flavour or style.

PINK GRAPEFRUIT & BASIL MOJITO

❶ INGREDIENTS

CASTER (SUPERFINE) SUGAR • LIME WEDGE
7 BASIL LEAVES • 2 TABLESPOONS DEMERARA SUGAR
150 ML (5 OZ) FRESHLY SQUEEZED PINK GRAPEFRUIT
JUICE • BASIL ICE CUBES, TO SERVE (SEE PAGE 30)
SODA WATER

❷ EQUIPMENT

TUMBLER   SMALL PLATE   MUDDLER

SERVES 1

This refreshing summer mocktail
has delicious sour notes. Freshly juiced
pink grapefruit gives off a lovely aroma.
Served in an elegant tumbler, this is a
very pretty drink.

❸ METHOD

Sprinkle a little caster sugar on to a plate.
Run the lime around the rim of the glass and
dip in the sugar. Put the basil leaves into the
glass with the demerara sugar and muddle.
Add the grapefruit juice and ice cubes, and
top up with soda water.

PUSSYFOOT

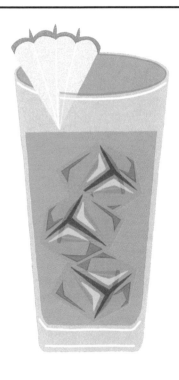

❶ INGREDIENTS

25 ML (1 OZ) CRANBERRY JUICE • 25 ML (1 OZ) APPLE JUICE • 50 ML (2 OZ) ORANGE JUICE • 50 ML (2 OZ) GRAPEFRUIT JUICE • JUICE OF 1 LEMON • LEMON ICE CUBES (SEE PAGE 30) • 1 PINEAPPLE WEDGE, TO GARNISH

❷ EQUIPMENT

HIGHBALL

SHAKER

❸ METHOD

Put all of the ingredients, except the pineapple wedge, into a cocktail shaker and shake vigorously. Pour into a glass and garnish with the pineapple wedge – make a small cut in the pineapple so it can sit on the rim.

SERVES 1
This is not an homage to an old pop act from the seventies, more of a comment on how you like to tread: a bit more carefully, with this tropical fruity drink.

GINGER & PEACH BELLINI

SERVES 1
A take on the Venetian summer fizz
that is made with prosecco. Try this
delicious alternative with non-alcoholic
spicy ginger beer.

❶ INGREDIENTS

½ WHITE PEACH, PEELED • 5 MM (¼ IN) THICK SLICE
GINGER, PEELED • 150 ML (5 OZ) CLOUDY GINGER BEER,
CHILLED • HANDFUL OF RASPBERRIES, PLUS EXTRA
TO GARNISH

❷ EQUIPMENT

SMALL BOWL   CHAMPAGNE   BLENDER   SIEVE
FLUTE

❸ METHOD

Purée the peach and ginger together with a
dash of water in the blender. Pour the purée into
champagne flutes and top each one with ginger
beer. Blitz the raspberries with a little water in
the blender, then push the pulp through a sieve
into a bowl to remove the seeds. Spoon the
raspberry purée on top of each drink, garnish
the glass with a raspberry and serve.

VIRGIN MARY

❶ INGREDIENTS

ICE CUBES • 150 ML (5 FL OZ) PASSATA • 1 TABLESPOON EACH OF WORCESTERSHIRE SAUCE AND LEMON JUICE 2 DROPS OF TABASCO SAUCE • PINCH EACH OF FRESHLY GROUND BLACK PEPPER, MUSTARD POWDER, CAYENNE PEPPER AND CELERY SALT • 1 TEASPOON GRATED HORSERADISH • ½ CELERY STICK AND SLICE OF LEMON, TO GARNISH

❷ EQUIPMENT

HIGHBALL GLASS   SHAKER   BLENDER

❸ METHOD

Crush enough ice cubes in a blender to fill the glass – don't over-blend or it will melt too quickly. Add the rest of the ingredients, except the celery stalk and slice of lemon, then tip everything into the cocktail shaker. Shake vigorously to combine, then pour back into the glass. Garnish with the celery and slice of lemon.

SERVES 1
This traditional non-alcoholic cocktail gives a good punch. Very similar to a Bloody Mary but without the vodka, our improved version gives it that little extra zip.

A MOCK OF GREEN

❶ INGREDIENTS

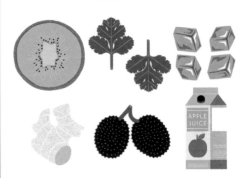

1 KIWI, PEELED AND CHOPPED, RESERVING 1 SLICE, TO GARNISH • 2.5 CM (1 IN) PIECE GINGER, PEELED • SMALL HANDFUL OF CORIANDER (CILANTRO) LEAVES • 75 ML (2½ OZ) LYCHEE JUICE • 75 ML (2½ OZ) APPLE JUICE • 4 ICE CUBES

❷ EQUIPMENT

HIGHBALL

BLENDER

❸ METHOD

Put all of the ingredients into a blender and pulse for 10–15 seconds until smooth. Pour into a glass and add a slice of kiwi to the top of the glass for a garnish.

SERVES 1
You can have green smoothies and green juices, so there is no reason why you can't have a green mocktail!

HEAVEN

❶ INGREDIENTS

140 ML (4½ OZ) LYCHEE JUICE • 4 ICE CUBES
3–4 GREEN GRAPES, HALVED • SODA WATER
2 TEASPOONS ROSE SYRUP

❷ EQUIPMENT

TUMBLER   SHAKER

❸ METHOD

SERVES 1
One can only imagine what it is like up there in floaty heaven – full of mellow-perfumed soft fruits combined with a little fizz perhaps!

Shake the lychee juice and ice together in a cocktail shaker, then pour into a tumbler. Add the halved grapes to the drink, top with soda water and drizzle with rose syrup.

BLONDIE

Elderflower cordial is delicious served on its own with some soda water and a slice of lemon peel. This recipe introduces lemongrass for an Asian twist.

SERVES 1

Ingredients
1 lemongrass, sliced, plus 1 lemongrass, to garnish
150 ml (5 oz) grape juice
2 tablespoons elderflower cordial
2–3 plain or grape ice cubes (see pages 30–31)
lemon peel, to serve

Equipment
Boston or pint glass, muddler, cocktail shaker, tea strainer or sieve, tumbler

Method
Put the sliced lemongrass into a glass and muddle. Add the grape juice, elderflower cordial and ice cubes. Secure the shaker over the top and shake vigorously. Strain into a tumbler and garnish with the lemon peel and lemongrass.

CRISP ENGLISH APPLE SANGRIA

The tartness of the verjuice – the juice from unripe grapes – and fizz of sparkling water in this sophisticated sangria will not leave you feeling soreheaded the next day; more likely you will have a feeling of pure joy! You can also serve this warm for a winter mocktail.

SERVES 4

Ingredients
300 ml (10 oz) verjuice
350 ml (12 oz) cloudy apple juice
25 ml (1 oz) ginger syrup
juice of 1 lemon
350 ml (12 oz) sparkling water
1 red apple, julienned
1 green apple, julienned
plain or viola ice cubes (see page 30)

Equipment
serving jug, wooden spoon, 4 tumblers

Method
Put all of the ingredients into a serving jug, adding enough ice to top the jug. Give everything a good stir and serve immediately in tumblers.

LEMON & LAVENDER GRANITA

This granita-style drink has a unique quality that will impress the most discerning of guests.

SERVES 4–6

Ingredients
625 ml (21 oz) water
200 ml (7 oz) honey
2½ tablespoons dried lavender
3 tablespoons lemon juice
4–6 slices of lemon, to serve

Equipment
saucepan, sieve, freezer-proof container, wooden spoon, fork, ice cream scoop, 4–6 small tumblers

Method
Simmer the water, honey and 1½ tablespoons lavender for 2–3 minutes, then cool. Strain into a freezer-proof container. Stir in the lemon juice and remaining lavender, then freeze. After 2 hours, remove from the freezer and use a fork to break up the mixture. Freeze for another hour, then repeat. Do so a further 3–4 times until you have fine ice crystals. Scoop into the tumblers. Serve each with a straw and a slice of lemon.

MINT & KIWI CAPRI

Coconut water has become a popular soft drink recently and lends itself well in this mocktail. A refreshing juicy taste with a mix of lime for a complex tongue tingle.

SERVES 1

Ingredients
1 kiwi, peeled and diced, reserving 1 slice, to serve
½ tablespoon granulated sugar
4 mint leaves, torn
juice of 1 lime
60 ml (2 oz) coconut water
crushed ice
sparkling water

Equipment
large tumbler, muddler

Method
Put the diced kiwi, sugar and mint leaves into the glass. Muddle together until the kiwi has become a coarse purée. Add the lime juice, coconut water and some crushed ice. Top up with sparkling water and stir. Add a straw and a slice of kiwi to serve.

JUICES

If you are after something refreshing without any fizz, you have come to the right chapter. These juices have the widest colour palette of all the drinks, from pink to green to dark purple to almost black. You can juice pretty much any fruit or veg on the planet. For an alternative option, add a bit of crushed ice and call it a slushy. Juicing has endless possibilities; try some of these to get you going.

WATERMELON JUICE

❶ INGREDIENTS

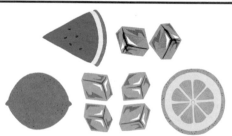

½ SMALL RIPE WATERMELON, DESEEDED AND DICED
JUICE OF ½ LIME • 4 PLAIN ICE CUBES
LIME ICE CUBES, TO SERVE (SEE PAGE 30)
2 SLICES OF LIME, TO SERVE

❷ EQUIPMENT

2 SMALL
TUMBLERS

METAL
SPOON

BLENDER

❸ METHOD

SERVES 2
Try to use a very ripe watermelon to bring out the natural sweetness in this refreshingly delicious juice.

Place the chopped watermelon into a blender. Whizz with the lime juice and plain ice until smooth. Pour into the tumblers, add a couple of lime ice cubes and garnish each glass with a slice of lime before serving.

GRAPEFRUIT, CUCUMBER & LIME

❶ INGREDIENTS

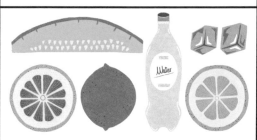

½ CUCUMBER, CHOPPED
1 GRAPEFRUIT, PEELED AND CHOPPED
1 LIME, PEELED AND PIPS REMOVED
200 ML (7 OZ) WATER • LIME ICE CUBES, TO SERVE
(SEE PAGE 30) • SLICE OF LIME, TO SERVE

❷ EQUIPMENT

TUMBLER   WOODEN SPOON   BLENDER   JUG   SIEVE

❸ METHOD

Put the cucumber, grapefruit, peeled lime and water into a blender and whizz until smooth. Pour the mixture through a sieve into a jug, helping the juice through using the back of a wooden spoon. Serve over some lime ice cubes in a tumbler, with a slice of lime.

SERVES 1

A real thirst quencher with sour notes, this juice is sure to wake up your taste buds!

BLACKBERRY, APPLE & MINT

SERVES 1
The English countryside in a glass.
Purple, fruity and tasty.

❶ INGREDIENTS

1 APPLE, CORED AND CHOPPED
150 G (5 OZ) BLACKBERRIES • 4 MINT LEAVES, PLUS EXTRA
TO SERVE • 100 ML (3½ OZ) WATER • MINT ICE CUBES, TO
SERVE (SEE PAGE 30)

❷ EQUIPMENT

TUMBLER BLENDER WOODEN JUG SIEVE
SPOON

❸ METHOD

Blend together the apple, blackberries, mint
leaves and water until smooth. Pour through
a sieve into a jug, helping the juice through
with the back of a wooden spoon. Pour into a
tumbler over mint ice cubes and garnish with
a sprig of mint.

GREEN TURBO

❶ INGREDIENTS

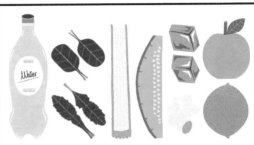

200 ML (7 OZ) WATER • HANDFUL OF KALE
HANDFUL OF SPINACH • 3 CELERY STICKS, CHOPPED
1 GREEN APPLE, CORED • 1 LEMON, PEELED AND PIPS
REMOVED • 2.5 CM (1 IN) PIECE GINGER
½ CUCUMBER, PLUS 1 SLICE, TO GARNISH
ICE CUBES, TO SERVE

❷ EQUIPMENT

TUMBLER BLENDER WOODEN JUG SIEVE
SPOON

❸ METHOD

SERVES 1
Every ounce of goodness you can get in
a glass – here it is.

Blend together all of the ingredients until
smooth. Push the mixture through a sieve into
a jug, helping it through with the back
of a wooden spoon. Pour into a tumbler over
ice, garnish with a slice of cucumber and soak
up the goodness!

PINEAPPLE & BASIL

Pineapple is such a fantastic fruit to make into a drink. Combined with basil, it really hits the spot.

SERVES 1

Ingredients
2 basil leaves
juice of ½ lime
½ pineapple, peeled and chopped,
  or 150 ml (5 oz) pineapple juice
slice of lime, to serve
lime ice cubes, to serve (see page 30)

Equipment
tumbler, muddler, blender, sieve, jug, wooden spoon

Method
Put the basil and lime juice into the bottom of the glass and muddle to combine the flavours. If you are using fresh pineapple, blitz the pieces in a blender until smooth. Pass the purée through a sieve into a jug, using a wooden spoon to help. Pour the pineapple juice into the basil and lime mixture. Top with ice cubes and garnish with a slice of lime.

MELON, PEACH & MINT

This juice is great in the summer when melons and peaches are at their ripest. Don't be shy with the mint!

SERVES 1

Ingredients
2 sprigs of mint, leaves picked,
  plus 1 extra sprig, to garnish
1 peach, peeled and de-stoned,
  reserving 1 slice, to serve
¼ cantaloupe melon, peeled and chopped
100 ml (3½ oz) water
ice cubes, to serve

Equipment
tumbler, muddler, blender, sieve, jug, wooden spoon

Method
Put the mint leaves into the bottom of a tumbler and muddle to extract their juices. Put the rest of the ingredients into a blender and blend until smooth. Push the mixture through a sieve into a jug using the back of a wooden spoon. Pour over the muddled mint and add a couple of ice cubes. Garnish with a sprig of mint.

BEETROOT, CARROT & GINGER

Surprisingly sweet with a delightful ginger kick, this dark juice is not only good for you but can be rather addictive once you get the taste for it.

SERVES 1

Ingredients
2 carrots, unpeeled, washed and roughly chopped
2 medium cooked beetroot, unpeeled, washed
 and quartered
2.5 cm (1 in) piece ginger, peeled
150 ml (5 oz) water
crushed ice cubes, to serve (optional)

Equipment
blender, sieve, jug, wooden spoon, slim Jim or tall glass

Method
Blend all the ingredients together until smooth. Push the mixture through a sieve into a jug using the back of a wooden spoon. Pour into a tall glass over crushed ice and serve immediately.

GREEN MELON CLEANSER

Healthy, enticing and tasty, this cleansing juice is a great way to start any day, or to perk you up whenever you feel you need a lift.

SERVES 1

Ingredients
½ cantaloupe melon, peeled and chopped
2 celery stalks, chopped
handful of rocket (arugula)
3 broccoli florets
handful of kale
1 kiwi, peeled and quartered,
 reserving 1 slice, to garnish
250 ml (8½ oz) water
lime ice cubes, to serve (see page 30)

Equipment
blender, sieve, jug, wooden spoon, slim Jim or tall glass

Method
Blend all the ingredients until smooth. Add extra water if the mixture is too thick, then push through a sieve into a jug using a wooden spoon. Pour into a tall glass over ice and serve with a slice of kiwi.

CARROT & SWEET POTATO

❶ INGREDIENTS

3 CARROTS, UNPEELED BUT WASHED
AND ROUGHLY CHOPPED
½ MEDIUM SWEET POTATO, PEELED AND CHOPPED
2 APPLES, CORED AND ROUGHLY CHOPPED
200 ML (7 OZ) WATER
CRUSHED ICE, TO SERVE (OPTIONAL)

❷ EQUIPMENT

SLIM JIM OR   WOODEN   BLENDER   JUG   SIEVE
TALL GLASS   SPOON

❸ METHOD

Put all of the ingredients into a blender and whizz until smooth. You can add a little more water if the consistency is too thick. Push the mixture through a sieve into a jug, using the back of a wooden spoon. Pour into a tall glass over crushed ice.

SERVES 1

This orange nectar is sweet and deliciously tasty. It's not often you drink a potato, so try it!

DETOXIFIER

❶ INGREDIENTS

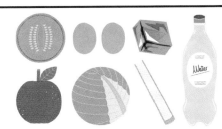

2 CELERY STALKS, CHOPPED, PLUS 1 EXTRA, TO SERVE
¼ GALIA MELON, PEELED AND CHOPPED
1 APPLE, CORED AND CHOPPED • HANDFUL OF
SEEDLESS GREEN GRAPES • ¼ GREEN CABBAGE,
CHOPPED • 200 ML (7 OZ) WATER • LIME ICE CUBES,
TO SERVE (SEE PAGE 30)

❷ EQUIPMENT

TUMBLER   WOODEN   BLENDER   JUG   SIEVE
SPOON

❸ METHOD

Blend all of the ingredients together until
smooth. If the consistency is too thick, add a
little more water. Push the mixture through
a sieve into a jug using the back of a wooden
spoon. Pour the juice into a tumbler, add lime
ice cubes and serve with a stick of celery
to garnish.

SERVES 1
If you're feeling under the weather, drink this
juice and it will give you a boost – it will make
you feel better and forget about any aches
and pains!

FRUITY
WATERS

Spice up your water by steeping it with fresh fruit and herbs. If cleansing the body and mind is what you need, try this selection of healthy drinks – there is nothing quite like cucumber water on a very hot day.

LEMON BARLEY WATER

MAKES APPROX. 1.5 LITRES (2½ PINTS)

This lemon barley water is so refreshing you will crave it every time the sun comes out. Serve thoroughly chilled.

❶ INGREDIENTS

65 g (2 oz) pearl barley
zest and juice of 2 lemons
1.5 litres (3 pints) water
110 g (4 oz) caster (superfine) sugar
1 lemon, sliced, to serve

❷ EQUIPMENT

SAUCEPAN   WOODEN SPOON   LARGE HEATPROOF BOWL   SIEVE   4–6 SLIM JIM OR TALL GLASSES

❸ METHOD

Put the pearl barley into a sieve and rinse it under cold running water until the water runs clear. Tip the barley into a saucepan along with the lemon zest and water. Slowly bring to the boil over a medium heat, then reduce the heat and simmer for 10 minutes. Pour the mixture through the sieve into a large heatproof bowl. Stir in the sugar and lemon juice and leave to cool. Cover the bowl with some cling film (plastic wrap) and refrigerate until chilled. Pour into tall slim glasses and add some slices of lemon to serve.

CUCUMBER, LIME & BASIL

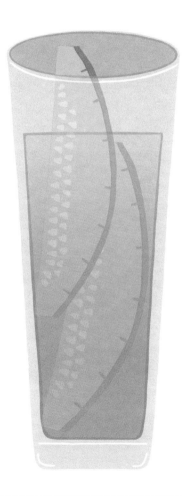

MAKES APPROX. 1.2 LITRES (2 PINTS)

Cool off with this infused water. The slight savouriness of the cucumber makes this drink a great non-alcoholic alternative to serve up with a meal.

❶ INGREDIENTS

1 cucumber
1 medium lime, sliced
handful of basil leaves
1 litre (34 oz) water

❷ EQUIPMENT

VEGETABLE PEELER   LARGE SERVING JUG   WOODEN SPOON   4 SLIM JIM OR TALL GLASSES

❸ METHOD

Use a vegetable peeler to make green stripes down the length of the cucumber leaving a stripe of skin between each peeling. Slice the cucumber and set aside a few slices to use as garnishes later. Put the rest of the cucumber along with the lime and basil leaves into the jug and softly mash them with the wooden spoon to release their juices. Top up with the water and refrigerate for a few hours, or overnight if possible. Pour into tall glasses and add a couple of cucumber slices to garnish.

STRAWBERRY & GRAPEFRUIT

Beautiful infused water not only tastes refreshing but looks a picture too.

MAKES APPROX. 1.5 LITRES (2½ PINTS)

❶ INGREDIENTS

1 pink grapefruit, cut in half

500 g (1 lb 2 oz) strawberries, hulled and halved

1.2 litres (2 pints) water

ice cubes, to serve

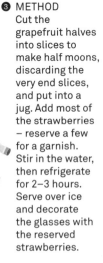

❷ EQUIPMENT
large serving jug, wooden spoon, tumblers

❸ METHOD
Cut the grapefruit halves into slices to make half moons, discarding the very end slices, and put into a jug. Add most of the strawberries – reserve a few for a garnish. Stir in the water, then refrigerate for 2–3 hours. Serve over ice and decorate the glasses with the reserved strawberries.

WATERMELON, CITRUS & MINT

Perky, pink and refreshing. This colourful infused water is perfect to slurp on summer days.

MAKES APPROX. 1.4 LITRES (2½ PINTS)

❶ INGREDIENTS

handful of mint leaves

2 limes

½ small watermelon, peeled, deseeded and diced

1.2 litres (2 pints) water

watermelon ice cubes, to serve (see pages 30-31)

❷ EQUIPMENT
large serving jug, muddler, tumblers

❸ METHOD
Put the mint into the jug and muddle. Slice 1 lime and add to the jug with the watermelon and water. Steep in the fridge for 2–3 hours, or overnight if possible. Pour into tumblers over watermelon ice and serve with slices of the remaining lime perched on the rim of each glass.

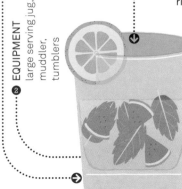

SPICED APPLE

This cinnamon-infused water has lots of things going for it, like boosting your immune system, smelling great and being wonderful for the skin!

MAKES APPROX. 1 LITRE (34 OZ)

❶ INGREDIENTS

1 red apple, cored and diced, plus extra slices, to garnish (optional)

1 green apple, cored and diced, plus extra slices, to garnish (optional)

1 cinnamon stick

1 litre (34 oz) water

ice cubes, to serve

❷ EQUIPMENT

large serving jug, tumblers

❸ METHOD
Add the diced apples, stick of cinnamon and water to the jug. Let the flavours steep for about 2 hours in the fridge. When ready to serve, put some ice cubes into each glass, pour over the infused water and garnish with a slice or two of apple, if you like.

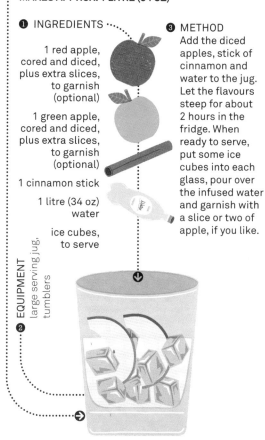

ZINGY CAYENNE WATER

Recommended for a morning wake-up drink, this spicy, zingy infused water gets the system going for a good day ahead.

MAKES APPROX. 650 ML (23 OZ)

❶ INGREDIENTS

½ cucumber

juice of 1 lemon

pinch of cayenne pepper

650 ml (23 oz) water

slices of lemon, to serve

❷ EQUIPMENT

vegetable peeler, large Mason jar or serving jug, wooden spoon, tumblers

❸ METHOD
Slice the cucumber into long thin strips with a vegetable peeler. Put into a Mason jar with the lemon juice, cayenne pepper and water. Screw on the lid and shake. (If using a jug, stir with a wooden spoon.) Steep for 1 hour in the fridge. Serve in tumblers with a slice of lemon in each.

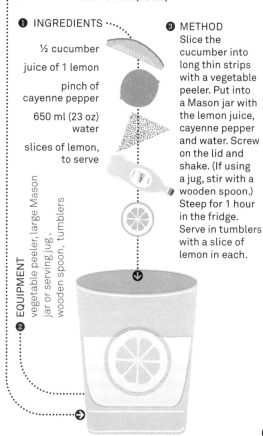

BLACKBERRY & ROSEMARY

❶ INGREDIENTS

300 G (10½ OZ) BLACKBERRIES, PLUS EXTRA TO SERVE
SPRIG OF ROSEMARY, PLUS EXTRA TO GARNISH
1 LITRE (34 OZ) WATER • ICE CUBES, TO SERVE

❷ EQUIPMENT

TUMBLERS   JUG   WOODEN SPOON

❸ METHOD

Put the blackberries and rosemary into a jug and muddle with the end of a wooden spoon. Pour in the water and let the flavours steep for 10–15 minutes in the fridge. Serve poured over ice cubes and blackberries in tumblers with a little sprig of rosemary to garnish.

MAKES APPROX. 1 LITRE (34 OZ)
A little bit of muddling makes this an instant infused water. Beautifully dark in colour, this can keep for up to three days in the fridge.

HONEYDEW, LIME & GINGER

❶ INGREDIENTS

½ HONEYDEW MELON, PEELED AND DICED
350 ML (12 OZ) COCONUT WATER • 2.5 CM (1 IN) PIECE
GINGER, PEELED • JUICE OF 1 LIME • LIME ICE CUBES,
TO SERVE (SEE PAGE 30) • SLICES OF LIME,
TO GARNISH • SPRIGS OF MINT, TO SERVE

❷ EQUIPMENT

JAM JARS BLENDER WOODEN JUG SIEVE
SPOON

❸ METHOD

Blend the melon, coconut water, ginger and lime juice together until smooth. Push the mixture through a sieve into a jug using a wooden spoon. Serve over lime ice cubes in jam jars, garnish with some slices of lime and sprigs of mint, and drink with a straw.

MAKES APPROX. 400 ML (14 OZ)
Fruity and tropical in flavour with a slight zing, this refreshing water will have you coming back for more.

CORIANDER & CITRUS WATER

❶ INGREDIENTS

ZEST AND JUICE OF 1 LEMON • 4 STEMS OF CORIANDER (CILANTRO), NO LEAVES • 1 TEASPOON CORIANDER SEEDS, SLIGHTLY CRUSHED
750 ML (25 OZ) WATER
1 LEMON, SLICED, TO SERVE

❷ EQUIPMENT

TUMBLERS   LARGE SERVING JUG

MAKES APPROX. 750 ML (25 OZ)
This drink goes wonderfully with Thai or Indian food, as it's both refreshing to drink and enhances the flavours of these cuisines. It's also a pretty drink to serve as the coriander (cilantro) stems go curly when left in liquid overnight in the fridge.

❸ METHOD

Add the lemon juice and zest, coriander stems and seeds, and water to the jug and leave to steep overnight in the fridge. Pour into tumblers and serve with a slice or two of lemon.

ORANGE, JUNIPER & BLUEBERRY

❶ INGREDIENTS

100 G (3½ OZ) BLUEBERRIES • 1 ORANGE, SLICED,
PLUS EXTRA TO GARNISH • 1 LEMON, SLICED
1 TEASPOON JUNIPER BERRIES, SLIGHTLY CRUSHED
750 ML (25 OZ) WATER • SPRIGS OF MINT, TO SERVE

❷ EQUIPMENT

TUMBLERS   LARGE
SERVING JUG

❸ METHOD

MAKES APPROX. 800 ML (28 OZ)
This water is a beautiful light pinky blue and
tastes really fruity. You can also use frozen
berries, if blueberries aren't in season.

Add all the ingredients except the extra
orange slices and sprigs of mint to the jug
and leave to steep for 6 hours in the fridge.
Pour into tumblers and garnish with a small
sprig of mint and a slice of orange on the rim
of each glass.

PUNCHES

Break the mould and create a little drama by adding an ice sculpture to your centrepiece. A punch should be full of fruit and fizziness, and served in a jug. Or, if you are really keen, in a huge bowl over an ice ring (see page 31). Not only should your punch look the part, but if you pop a ladle in it, people can help themselves.

CARROT & ORANGE BLOSSOM COOLER

❶ INGREDIENTS

4 CARROTS, PEELED AND ROUGHLY CHOPPED
2 ORANGES, PEELED AND PIPS REMOVED
100 ML (3½ OZ) WATER • JUICE OF 1 LEMON
½ TEASPOON ORANGE BLOSSOM WATER • CRUSHED
ICE, TO SERVE • VIOLAS OR OTHER EDIBLE FLOWERS,
TO GARNISH (OPTIONAL)

❷ EQUIPMENT

TUMBLER   WOODEN   BLENDER   JUG   SIEVE
          SPOON

❸ METHOD

MAKES APPROX. 400 ML (13 OZ)
This punch is reminiscent of spring, with its
bright fresh colours and light floral taste.
Great for a crowd and to start off the evening.

Blend the carrots, oranges and water together
until smooth. Push the mixture through a sieve
into a jug using a wooden spoon. Stir in the
lemon juice and orange blossom water. Add
some crushed ice to each tumbler, pour over the
cooler and top with an edible flower to garnish.

COCONUT, WATERMELON & LIME PUNCH

❶ INGREDIENTS

½ SMALL WATERMELON, PEELED AND DICED
10 MINT LEAVES • JUICE OF 2 LIMES
500 ML (17 OZ) COCONUT WATER
LIME ICE CUBES, TO SERVE (SEE PAGE 30)
250 ML (8½ OZ) SODA WATER

❷ EQUIPMENT

TUMBLERS   BLENDER

❸ METHOD

MAKES APPROX. 900 ML (31 OZ)
Tropical punch with a sophisticated flavour of sweet watermelon and tasty coconut!

Blitz the watermelon, mint leaves, lime juice and coconut water together in a blender until smooth. Add a couple of ice cubes to each tumbler, fill the glass to three-quarters full with the watermelon mixture, then top up with soda water. Serve immediately.

SPICED PEARADE

Big on flavours and full of complexity, this punch will be the talk of the night.

MAKES APPROX. 900 ML (31 OZ)

Ingredients
6 pears, peeled, cored and chopped, reserving
  some thin slices to garnish
1½ tablespoons light brown sugar
½ teaspoon ground cinnamon
juice of ½ lemon
350 ml (12 oz) verjuice or white grape juice
400 ml (13 oz) sparkling water
ice cubes, to serve

Equipment
mixing bowl, baking sheet lined with baking parchment, large spoon, blender, sieve, large punch bowl, tumblers

Method
Preheat the grill (broiler). Toss together the pears, sugar and cinnamon in a mixing bowl then tip the pears on to the baking sheet. Grill for 4 minutes, turning halfway. Blitz the pears in a blender with the lemon juice and verjuice. Sieve into a punch bowl then chill for 1 hour. Fill each tumbler halfway, add sparkling water and ice. Serve with a slice of pear.

MELON BALL PUNCH

Summertime has arrived, with tart lime and colourful melon balls.

MAKES APPROX. 1.2 LITRES (2 PINTS)

Ingredients
700 ml (24 oz) verjuice or white grape juice
250 ml (8½ oz) lemonade
½ each of small watermelon, cantaloupe
  melon and honeydew melon
10 mint leaves
3 limes, sliced

Equipment
large punch bowl, melon baller, baking tray lined with baking parchment, wooden spoon, large tumblers

Method
Pour the verjuice and lemonade into a bowl and chill. Scoop out the flesh from the melons and place on a lined tray that can fit in the freezer. Freeze for 2 hours. Add handfuls of frozen melon balls to the bowl with the mint and two-thirds of the lime slices and stir; return the reserved melon balls to the freezer. Refrigerate the punch for 30 minutes. Pop frozen melon balls into each glass, pour over the punch and serve with the remaining lime slices.

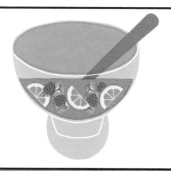

RASPBERRY SORBET & GINGER ALE PUNCH

Wow... this is definitely a party punch, full of raspberries popping with flavour.

MAKES APPROX. 1.2 LITRES (2 PINTS)

Ingredients
175 ml (6 oz) lemon juice
115 ml (4 oz) orange juice
460 ml (15½ oz) ginger ale, chilled
425 g (14¼ oz) raspberry sorbet
400 g (15 oz) raspberries
slices of orange, halved, to serve
raspberry ice cubes, to serve (see pages 30–31)

Equipment
large punch bowl or serving jug, wooden spoon, ice cream scoop, tumblers, ladle

Method
Pour the lemon juice, orange juice and ginger ale into a punch bowl or jug and stir to combine. Scoop balls of the raspberry sorbet and add them to the bowl, then sprinkle the raspberries into the bowl too. Add a slice of orange to each tumbler along with a few ice cubes then ladle the punch into the glasses and serve.

TRADITIONAL FRUIT PUNCH

This is great to serve in a large punch bowl with a homemade frozen ring to impress guests; you will need to leave the ring overnight to freeze so make sure you make it the day before your party.

MAKES APPROX. 1 LITRE (34 OZ)

Ingredients
400 ml (13 oz) orange juice
150 ml (5 oz) pineapple juice
150 ml (5 oz) pomegranate or cranberry juice
300 ml (10 oz) soda water
seeds of 1 pomegranate
1 orange, sliced

For the frozen ring
400 ml (13 oz) orange juice
150 ml (5 oz) pineapple juice
150 ml (5 oz) pomegranate or cranberry juice

Equipment
freezer-proof Bundt tin or mould, large punch bowl, wooden spoon, ladle, tumblers

Method
Make the frozen ring (see page 31). Place the frozen ring in a punch bowl. Add all the punch ingredients to the bowl and stir. Ladle the punch into tumblers and serve.

ELDERFLOWER FIZZ WITH BORAGE

A punch to dress up for – it looks and feels sophisticated; a great alternative for non-champagne drinkers.

MAKES 850 ML (29 OZ)

❶ INGREDIENTS ⋯

1 unwaxed lemon, to serve

sprigs of borage, to serve

crushed ice to, serve

100 ml (3½ oz) elderflower cordial or syrup

750 ml (25 oz) sparkling water, chilled

❷ EQUIPMENT vegetable peeler, large serving jug, champagne flutes

❸ METHOD
Shave slivers of lemon peel from the lemon using a vegetable peeler. Put a piece into each champagne flute along with a sprig of borage and a little crushed ice. Mix the elderflower and water together in a jug, then slowly pour it into the flutes and serve.

STRAWBERRY PUNCH WITH TAMARIND

A tangy, tasty punch, which is rich in colour. Tamarind gives this a distinct sweet-sour flavour, with an umami lift.

MAKES APPROX. 750 ML (25 OZ)

❶ INGREDIENTS ⋯

200 g (7 oz) strawberries

3–4 sprigs of basil

1 tablespoon tamarind paste

juice of 1 lime

3 tablespoons sugar syrup

750 ml (25 oz) sparkling water

strawberry ice cubes, to serve (see pages 30–31)

❷ EQUIPMENT large serving jug, wooden spoon, tall glasses

❸ METHOD
Hull and thinly slice the strawberries and pick the leaves from the basil. Put all the ingredients into a jug and stir. Chill for 1 hour. Fill tall glasses with strawberry ice cubes, pour over the punch and serve.

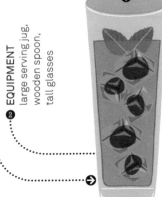

SPARKLING BLUEBERRY PUNCH

A beautifully-coloured purple punch!

MAKES APPROX. 1 LITRE (34 OZ)

❶ INGREDIENTS

800g (1 lb 12 oz) blueberries, plus extra to garnish

550 ml (18½ oz) water

230 ml (8 oz) lemon juice

150g (5 oz) caster (superfine) sugar

40 ml (1½ oz) elderflower cordial

mint ice cubes (see page 31), to serve

sparkling water

❷ EQUIPMENT blender, sieve, jug, wooden spoon, mixing bowl, tumblers

❸ METHOD
Blend the blueberries with 100 ml (3½ oz) water until smooth then push through a sieve into a jug. Stir the lemon juice, sugar, elderflower and remaining water in a bowl. Tip into the blueberry juice and chill for 1 hour. Serve in tumblers with ice cubes, topped up with sparkling water. Garnish, with blueberries.

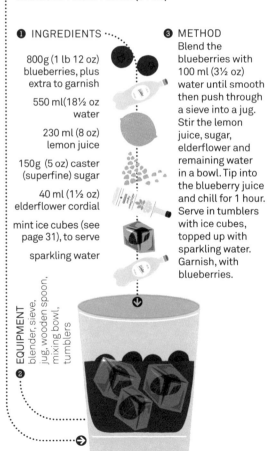

TRADITIONAL LEMONADE

There's nothing like fresh lemonade on a hot summer's day. The little effort this takes is well worth it.

MAKES APPROX. 1.4 LITRES (2½ PINTS)

❶ INGREDIENTS

1.4 litres (2½ pints) water

zest and juice of 3 unwaxed lemons

150 g (5 oz) granulated sugar

ice cubes, to serve

soda water, (optional)

slices of lemon, to serve

sprigs of mint, to serve

❷ EQUIPMENT kettle, heatproof jug, wooden spoon, sieve, jug, tall glasses

❸ METHOD
Boil the water and pour it into a heatproof jug over the lemon zest, juice and sugar. Stir to combine then leave overnight to cool. Give everything another stir and check the taste; if you feel it needs to be slightly sweeter, add a little more sugar. Strain the lemonade through a sieve into a serving jug and refrigerate. Serve in tall glasses with lots of ice and a dash of soda water if you fancy some fizz. Garnish with slices of lemon and sprigs of mint.

SHAKES

These sweet-tasting, ice cream-flavoured, colourfully decorated long drinks are just what your blender needs. Not only great after a meal, but they're packed with a multitude of amazing ingredients. What's your favourite biscuit – custard cream? Try it in a shake…

BANOFFEE MILKSHAKE

If you love bananas then this shake is for you!

SERVES 1

Ingredients
2 ripe bananas, peeled and sliced
250 ml (8½ oz) whole or semi-skimmed milk
2 scoops caramel or vanilla fudge ice cream
1 teaspoon lemon juice
1 teaspoon honey (optional)
grated chocolate, to serve

Equipment
blender
tall glass

Method
Put most of the sliced bananas into the blender – reserve a few slices to serve – along with the milk, ice cream and lemon juice. Blitz until smooth. Check the taste and if you would like it sweeter add the honey and pulse for a few seconds more. Pour into tall glasses, garnish with the remaining banana slices and sprinkle over the grated chocolate to serve.

CUSTARD CREAM SHAKE

A childhood favourite biscuit turned into a milkshake – yum!

SERVES 4

Ingredients
12 custard cream biscuits
2 tablespoons custard powder
500 ml (17 oz) skimmed or semi-skimmed milk
4 scoops vanilla ice cream

Equipment
blender
4 tumblers

Method
Put 10 of the custard creams into a blender along with the custard powder and pulse for a few seconds. Add 100 ml (3½ oz) of the milk and blend to loosen the mixture. Pour in the rest of the milk and blend until smooth. Put a scoop of ice cream into each tumbler and pour over the milkshake. Split the remaining custard creams in half and stick half into the ice cream in each glass, then serve.

CHOCOLATE OATY SHAKE

For those who love an oaty biscuit with the added indulgence of chocolate.

SERVES 2

Ingredients
11 chocolate Hobnobs or other chocolate oat
 biscuits
500 ml (17 oz) semi-skimmed milk
2 scoops vanilla ice cream

Equipment
blender
2 large tumblers

Method
Break 10 of the Hobnobs into a blender and pulse for 30 seconds. Add 100 ml (3½ oz) of the milk and blend to loosen the mixture. Pour in the rest of the milk and blitz until smooth. Add a scoop of vanilla ice cream to each tumbler, pour over the milkshake. Split the remaining Hobnob in half and stick one half in each ice crem, then serve.

COFFEE MILKSHAKE

This can be made as strong as you like to suit your coffee taste and you can omit the sugar if you prefer.

SERVES 2

Ingredients
4 shots espresso, cooled
200 ml (7 oz) semi-skimmed milk
1 teaspoon sugar (optional)
4 scoops vanilla ice cream
whipped cream, to serve
chocolate-covered espresso beans, to serve

Equipment
jug
wooden spoon
2 tumblers

Method
Pour the coffee into a jug and stir in the milk and sugar. Add 2 scoops of ice cream to each tumbler then pour over the coffee mixture. Spoon or squirt some whipped cream into the top of each glass, sprinkle over a few chocolate-covered espresso beans and serve.

CHERRY & CHOCOLATE MILKSHAKE

A winning combination of cherries with chocolate mixed with ice cream just to top it off! Waistlines... forget about those!

SERVES 2

❶ INGREDIENTS

180 ml (6 oz) semi-skimmed milk

80 ml (2¾ oz) chocolate syrup

10 maraschino cherries, stems removed from 8

4 scoops vanilla ice cream

whipped cream, to serve

❸ METHOD
Put the milk, chocolate syrup, the 8 stemless cherries and the ice cream into a blender and whizz until smooth. Pour into 2 tumblers, top with whipped cream and a cherry, and serve.

❷ EQUIPMENT
blender, 2 tumblers

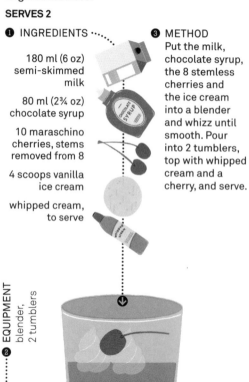

NUTTY VANILLA BEAN SHAKE

This shake, loved by adults and children alike, uses cashew butter to pimp it up.

SERVES 2

❶ INGREDIENTS

4 scoops vanilla ice cream

180 ml (6 oz) semi-skimmed milk

1 teaspoon vanilla extract

4 tablespoons cashew nut butter

caramelised cashew nuts, to garnish

❸ METHOD
Blend the ice cream, milk, vanilla extract and nut butter until smooth. Pour into each tumbler, top with a few caramelised cashew nuts to garnish and drink with a straw.

❷ EQUIPMENT
blender, 2 tumblers

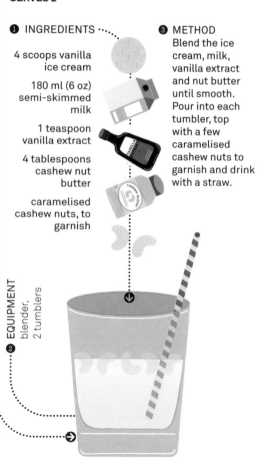

CLASSIC BANANA SHAKE

Who doesn't love a banana milkshake? This combines real bananas with a caramel sauce.

SERVES 2

❶ INGREDIENTS ⋯

2 bananas, peeled and sliced

4 scoops vanilla ice cream

180 ml (6 oz) semi-skimmed milk

2 tablespoons dulce de leche or caramel sauce, plus extra to serve

whipped cream, to serve

❷ EQUIPMENT
blender,
2 large tumblers

❸ METHOD
Put most of the banana in a blender, reserving a few slices to use as a garnish. Add the ice cream, milk and caramel sauce and blend until smooth. Pour the milkshake into tumblers, top with some whipped cream and the reserved banana slices, and finish with a drizzle of caramel sauce.

PEACH MELBA SHAKE

This was one of the best and most popular desserts in the eighties, and now you can make it into a shake to bring back all those wonderful memories.

SERVES 2

❶ INGREDIENTS ⋯

handful of raspberries

1 tin sliced peaches, drained (drained weight approx. 240 g/ 8½ oz)

4 scoops vanilla ice cream

180 ml (6 oz) semi-skimmed milk

¼ teaspoon almond extract

❷ EQUIPMENT
blender, sieve, small bowl, spoon, 2 tumblers

❸ METHOD
Make the raspberry purée by blending the raspberries with a dash of water then pass through a sieve with a spoon, into a bowl to remove the seeds. Rinse the blender then add the rest of the ingredients and blitz until smooth. Pour into 2 glasses and drizzle over the raspberry purée.

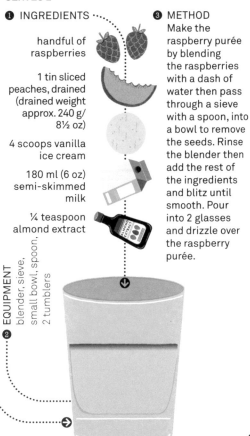

CAKE MIX SHAKE

❶ INGREDIENTS

RUNNY HONEY • HUNDREDS AND THOUSANDS (SUGAR SPRINKLES) • 3 SCOOPS VANILLA ICE CREAM 220 ML (8 OZ) MILK • 115 G (4 OZ) VANILLA SPONGE CAKE MIX (AVAILABLE FROM MOST SUPERMARKETS)

❷ EQUIPMENT

2 TALL GLASSES 2 SMALL PLATES BLENDER

❸ METHOD

Squeeze a little runny honey on to a small plate and sprinkle some hundreds and thousands (sugar sprinkles) on to another plate. Dip the rim of each glass first into the honey and then into the hundreds and thousands to decorate them. Blend the rest of the ingredients until smooth, then carefully pour the shake into the glasses and serve.

SERVES 2
Some might say this is unusual, while to others this is awesome! Sometimes licking the cake mix from the bowl is the best bit about it.

CREAMY LEMON SHAKE

❶ INGREDIENTS

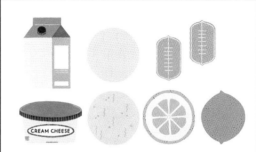

2 LEMON SHERBETS, CRUSHED IN A PESTLE
AND MORTAR • ½ LEMON • 180 ML (6 OZ) SEMI-SKIMMED
MILK • 2 SCOOPS VANILLA ICE CREAM
2 SCOOPS LEMON SORBET • 100 G (3½ OZ) CREAM CHEESE
2 TEASPOONS LEMON ZEST

❷ EQUIPMENT

2 LARGE   SMALL PLATE   BLENDER
TUMBLERS

❸ METHOD

SERVES 2
If you like your shakes to be a little bit
more tart, try this one for size.

Tip the crushed lemon sherbets on to a plate.
Run the halved lemon around the rim of each
glass, then dip the rim into the lemon sherbet
powder to decorate the glasses. Blend the rest of
the ingredients until smooth, then carefully pour
the shake into the glasses and serve.

SEASONAL

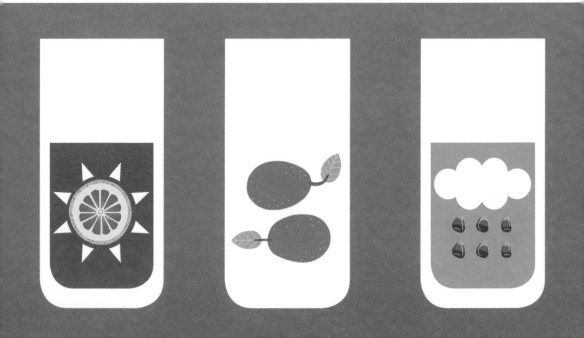

Springtime: the birds are singing, the flowers are starting to open – let's mark it with a drink. Summer: it's hot, your taste buds crave barbecued food and picnics... but what to drink? Festive cheer is here – what alternative Christmas fizz can be consumed? All the best drinks to complement any given season are here, so you don't need to go anywhere else!

WINTER: SATSUMA & CRANBERRY FESTIVE FIZZ

❶ INGREDIENTS

JUICE OF 5 SATSUMAS
200 ML (7 OZ) CRANBERRY JUICE
2 TABLESPOONS ROSEMARY SYRUP
ICE CUBES, TO SERVE
450 ML (15½ OZ) SODA WATER
4 SMALL SPRIGS OF ROSEMARY, TO GARNISH

❷ EQUIPMENT

4 TUMBLERS   JUG   SPOON

❸ METHOD

SERVES 4

'Tis the season to bring out some colourful fizz with tangy fruits. The rosemary syrup teases with a savoury note.

Stir the satsuma juice, cranberry juice and rosemary syrup together in a jug. Divide the mixture between the tumblers, add ice cubes to each glass and top up with the soda water. Add a small sprig of rosemary to garnish and serve.

WINTER: CHRISTMAS ORANGE NOG

❶ INGREDIENTS

4 ORANGES, PEELED, QUARTERED
230 ML (8 OZ) UNSWEETENED ALMOND MILK
2 HANDFULS OF ICE, PLUS EXTRA FOR SERVING
5 DROPS ORANGE BLOSSOM WATER
½ TEASPOON VANILLA EXTRACT
1 TABLESPOON HONEY

❷ EQUIPMENT

2 TUMBLERS   BLENDER

❸ METHOD

SERVES 2
This delicious orange drink is a perfect
morning pick-me-up during winter.

Add all of the ingredients to the blender and
blitz until smooth. Put some ice into each
tumbler and pour over the nog before serving.

SPRING: KUMQUAT & PINK PEPPERCORN FIZZ

● INGREDIENTS

115 ML (4 OZ) WATER • 115 G (4 OZ) CASTER (SUPERFINE) SUGAR • 1 TEASPOON PINK PEPPERCORNS, LIGHTLY CRUSHED, PLUS EXTRA TO GARNISH 12 KUMQUATS, SLICED INTO ROUNDS AND SEEDS REMOVED • ICE CUBES, TO SERVE SODA WATER, TO SERVE

❷ EQUIPMENT

SAUCEPAN   6 TUMBLERS   JUG   MUDDLER   SIEVE

❸ METHOD

SERVES 6
This drink pops with colours and flavours to excite anyone's palate.

Simmer the water and sugar in a saucepan. Off the heat, stir in the peppercorns and set aside for 30 minutes. Strain into a jug then cool. Divide the kumquat between the glasses and muddle. Stir 2 tablespoons of pepper syrup into each glass, add ice cubes, top up with soda water and garnish with peppercorns.

SPRING: SPRING PEA & ELDERFLOWER 'TAIL

SERVES 2
This is the epitome of spring in a glass, with muddled fresh peas and fragrant elderflower.

❶ INGREDIENTS

4 TABLESPOONS FRESH PEAS, BLANCHED
2 TABLESPOONS CHOPPED CUCUMBER
1 TEASPOON CASTER (SUPERFINE) SUGAR
ICE CUBES • 2 TABLESPOONS ELDERFLOWER CORDIAL
TONIC WATER • PEA ICE CUBES (SEE PAGES 30–31),
LEMON WEDGES AND TARRAGON SPRIGS, TO SERVE

❷ EQUIPMENT

4 BOSTON OR   STRAINER   MUDDLER   SHAKER
PINT GLASSES

❸ METHOD

Divide the peas, cucumber and sugar between the glasses and muddle. Add ice cubes, elderflower cordial and tonic water. Secure the cocktail shaker over a glass and shake. Strain over pea ice cubes in a glass. Repeat. Serve with lemon wedges and tarragon sprigs.

SPRING: RHUBARB & THYME

❶ INGREDIENTS

200 ML (7 OZ) RHUBARB SYRUP
750 ML (25 OZ) SPARKLING WATER
1 ORANGE, TO SERVE
6 LONG SPRIGS OF THYME, TO GARNISH

❷ EQUIPMENT

VEGETABLE   JUG   6 CHAMPAGNE   WOODEN
PEELER   FLUTES   SPOON

❸ METHOD

Mix the rhubarb syrup and sparkling water together in a jug and give it a stir. Use a vegetable peeler to make slivers of orange peel from the orange and add 1 or 2 pieces to each glass. Pour the rhubarb fizz into each flute and garnish with the sprigs of thyme.

SERVES 6
When in season, rhubarb is delicious, so it would be a great shame not to honour its flavour in a glass. Celebrate spring in style.

SUMMER: SUMMER CHERRY & GINGER SODA

❶ INGREDIENTS

120 G (4 OZ) PITTED CHERRIES,
PLUS 4 WHOLE CHERRIES TO GARNISH
JUICE OF ½ LIME
85 ML (2½ OZ) ELDERFLOWER CORDIAL
1 TABLESPOON GINGER SYRUP
CRUSHED ICE, TO SERVE
340 ML (11½ OZ) GINGER BEER

❷ EQUIPMENT

4 TALL GLASSES   BLENDER

SERVES 4
Ginger beer is delicious on its own, but adding a little summery fruit to it brings out its flavour even more.

❸ METHOD

Blend together the pitted cherries, lime juice, elderflower cordial and ginger syrup until smooth. Fill each glass with crushed ice and pour over the cherry juice. Top up with ginger beer and garnish with a whole cherry.

WINTER: SPICED GINGER WINTER SODA

❶ INGREDIENTS

180 G (6 OZ) CASTER (SUPERFINE) SUGAR • 2 TEASPOONS
CRUSHED CHILLI FLAKES • PINCH OF SALT
4 CM (1½ IN) PIECE GINGER, PEELED
AND FINELY CHOPPED • ICE CUBES, TO SERVE
230 ML (8 OZ) WATER • SODA WATER, TO SERVE
LIME WEDGES, TO SERVE

❷ EQUIPMENT

SAUCEPAN   6 TUMBLERS   JUG   LONG SPOON   SIEVE

❸ METHOD

SERVES 6
Something special to warm you from
the inside!

Bring the sugar, chilli, salt, ginger and water
to the boil in a saucepan over a medium heat,
then simmer for 10 minutes. Remove from the
heat. Leave to infuse for 30 minutes. Strain into
a jug. Add 2 tablespoons of the syrup to each
glass, with ice and a splash of soda water. Stir to
combine and serve with a lime wedge.

AUTUMN: PINK GRAPEFRUIT & POM SODA

❶ INGREDIENTS

115 ML (4 OZ) PINK GRAPEFRUIT JUICE
115 ML (4 FL Z) POMEGRANATE JUICE
230 G (8 OZ) CASTER (SUPERFINE) SUGAR
2 STAR ANISE • CRUSHED ICE, TO SERVE • SODA WATER,
TO SERVE • POMEGRANATE SEEDS, TO SERVE

❷ EQUIPMENT

SAUCEPAN   6 TALL GLASSES   SPOON

❸ METHOD

Boil the juices, sugar and star anise in a
saucepan for 1 minute. Remove from the heat
and leave for 30 minutes to cool completely.
Remove the star anise with a spoon. Fill each
glass halfway with crushed ice, then add
3 tablespoons of syrup, soda water and a
scattering of pomegranate seeds.

SERVES 6
Spiced with hints of liquorice, this vivid fizz
is unusual and quite grown up.

ENERGIZERS

Why don't you pump it up a little more with these thirst-quenching, body-building, energy-fuelling game changers. Or perhaps just try one pre- or post-workout, sporting match or swimathon!

THE BEETROOT

This veg is the best thing to perk you up and give you an extra skip in your step without a drop of caffeine.

SERVES 1

Ingredients
1 apple, unpeeled, washed, cored and roughly
 chopped
2 carrots, unpeeled, washed and roughly chopped
2.5 cm (1 in) piece ginger, peeled
2 beetroot, unpeeled, washed and roughly
 chopped
4 mint leaves, plus 1 sprig to garnish
juice of ½ lemon
250 ml (8½ oz) water

Equipment
blender, sieve, jug, wooden spoon,
slim Jim or tall glass

Method
Blend all of the ingredients together except the sprig of mint until smooth. Push the juice through a sieve into a jug using the back of a wooden spoon. Pour into a glass and garnish with a sprig of mint.

GREEN CHIA SEED PICK-ME-UP

Full of health benefits, this energy-boosting green tea is a great workout drink.

SERVES 1

Ingredients
230 ml (8 oz) water
1 green tea bag
1 tablespoon chia seeds

Equipment
kettle, heatproof jug, tall glass

Method
Boil the water then pour it over the teabag in the jug and let it steep for 3–5 minutes. Remove the teabag, add the chia seeds and mix thoroughly. Cool a little then transfer to the fridge and leave for 1 hour to cool. Give the tea a stir before pouring it into a tall glass. Drink immediately.

ELECTROLYTE CITRUS

This natural sports drink rehydrates your system, making you feel tip top and ready to go.

SERVES 2

Ingredients
115 ml (4 oz) freshly squeezed orange juice
80 ml (2½ oz) freshly squeezed lemon juice
450 ml (15½ oz) water
2 tablespoons honey
pinch of salt
2 slices of lemon or orange, to serve

Equipment
jug, wooden spoon, 2 tall glasses

Method
Add all of the ingredients, except for the orange or lemon slices, in a jug and mix well using a wooden spoon. Put a slice of lemon or orange into each of the glasses, pour over the juice and serve.

TROPICAL COCONUT

This body refresher drink hits all the right spots. The ginger helps to stimulate blood circulation, which will pick you up if you're at a low ebb.

SERVES 1

Ingredients
180 ml (6 oz) pineapple juice
120 ml (4 oz) coconut water
1 tablespoon ginger syrup
juice of 1 lime
plain ice cubes
lime ice cubes, to serve (see page 30)

Equipment
Boston or pint glass, cocktail shaker,
large tumbler, strainer

Method
Put the pineapple juice, coconut water, ginger syrup and lime juice into a Boston or pint glass along with a few plain ice cubes. Secure the cocktail shaker on top of the glass and give it a good shake for 1 minute. Add the lime ice cubes to a tumbler and pour the cooled shaken juice into the glass through a strainer.

ICED GREEN TEA

❶ INGREDIENTS

100 ML (3½ OZ) WATER • 1 GREEN TEA BAG
2 MINT LEAVES • HANDFUL OF BLUEBERRIES
1 TABLESPOON AGAVE SYRUP• 120 ML (4 OZ)
POMEGRANATE JUICE • JUICE OF ½ LEMON
ICE CUBES, TO SERVE

❷ EQUIPMENT

KETTLE   HEATPROOF   TUMBLER   MUDDLER
          JUG

❸ METHOD

Boil the water then pour it over the tea bag in a heatproof jug and let it steep for 3 minutes. Remove tea bag and leave for about 1 hour to cool. Put the mint leaves, blueberries and agave into a glass and muddle to release their flavours. Pour the pomegranate juice and lemon juice over the blueberry mixture, then top up with the tea. Add ice cubes and serve.

SERVES 1
An iced tea full of energizing fruit. Tasty!

CHOCOLATE 'SPRESSO

❶ INGREDIENTS

1 TEASPOON CACAO NIBS
1 SHOT OF ESPRESSO
150 ML (5 OZ) MILK
1 TEASPOON AGAVE SYRUP
1 PINCH OF CAYENNE PEPPER
ICE CUBES, TO SERVE

❷ EQUIPMENT

HEATPROOF JUG   TUMBLER   SPOON

❸ METHOD

SERVES 1
This super energising mocha choca spiced up coffee is all you need to embrace the day ahead.

Put the cacao nibs into a jug and add your hot espresso. Stir the nibs until melted. Now add the milk, syrup and cayenne and stir again. Pour into a tumbler, add ice cubes and serve.

15

HOT DRINKS

Perhaps you have some friends staying, or the kids have come in from the cold. Try these hot and enticing drinks to warm everybody up from the inside. Whip up some cream or add a marshmallow or two for soft, fluffy madness.

HOT MARSHMALLOW MILK

SERVES 2

This cuddle in a cup is so comforting, and it almost tastes like warm vanilla ice cream.

① INGREDIENTS

460 ml (15½ oz) whole milk
40 g (1½ oz) light brown sugar
pinch of salt
1 teaspoon vanilla extract
marshmallows, to serve

② EQUIPMENT

SAUCEPAN

2 MUGS

WOODEN SPOON

③ METHOD

Add all of the ingredients apart from the marshmallows to a saucepan and slowly bring up to a simmer, gently stirring occasionally to help dissolve the sugar. When all the sugar has dissolved, take the pan off the heat. Pour the hot vanilla milk into the mugs, top with marshmallows and serve.

HOT CHOCOLATE PEANUT BUTTER

SERVES 2

This is a love-it-or-hate-it combination, so for those who hate peanut butter, read no further and move on. Those of you who love it, stay here and dive right in!

❶ INGREDIENTS

500 ml (17 oz) whole (full-fat) milk
2 teaspoons cornflour (cornstarch)
2 teaspoons cocoa powder
50 g (2 oz) milk chocolate chips
2 tablespoons dark chocolate chips
3 heaped tablespoons smooth peanut butter
whipped cream, to serve
chocolate syrup, to serve
handful of peanuts, to serve

❷ EQUIPMENT

SMALL BOWL   SAUCEPAN   WHISK   2 MUGS

❸ METHOD

Put 2 tablespoons of the milk into a small bowl and whisk in the cornflour. Pour the rest of the milk into a saucepan along with the cocoa powder, chocolate chips and peanut butter. Whisk continuously over a medium heat until the chocolate and peanut butter have melted and the milk is steaming hot – don't allow the milk to boil. Pour in the cornflour mixture and whisk together. Continue to heat gently for 1 minute to allow the milk to thicken slightly. Pour into the mugs and serve with whipped cream, chocolate syrup and a sprinkling of peanuts.

HOT 'BENA AND LIME

SERVES 1

Invented in 1938, blackcurrant Ribena has been a childhood favourite for generations and so has comforting connotations for many people. Usually drunk cold, here we make it hot – lovely to help soothe a sore throat.

❶ INGREDIENTS

225 ml (8 oz) water
1½ tablespoons Ribena cordial or other
  blackcurrant cordial
¼ lime

❷ EQUIPMENT

KETTLE   MUG

❸ METHOD

Boil the water in a kettle. Pour the Ribena into a mug, squeeze in the juice from the lime and drop the lime into the mug too. Pour over the boiling water and serve.

HONEY & LEMON

SERVES 1

Many say this is a medicinal drink, and particularly great for a tickly cough. Whether for medicinal purposes or not, this is a lovely soothing hot drink for all.

❶ INGREDIENTS

225 ml (8 oz) water
½ lemon
1 tablespoon honey
slice of lemon, to serve

❷ EQUIPMENT

KETTLE   MUG   SPOON

❸ METHOD

Boil the water in the kettle. Squeeze the juice from the lemon into a mug and drop the lemon into the mug too. Add the honey and pour over the boiling water. Stir and serve.

MOCHA COFFEE

Very special coffee made with real hot chocolate and cream. Mmm.

SERVES 1

Ingredients
110 g (4 oz) whole (full-fat) milk
30 g (1 oz) grated dark chocolate
brown sugar, to taste
115 ml (4 oz) strong coffee
50 ml (2 oz) double (heavy) cream, whisked
chocolate shavings, to garnish

Equipment
small bowl, whisk, large glass mug, tablespoon

Method
Make the hot chocolate by bringing the milk to a simmer and whisking in the grated chocolate and the brown sugar until fully melted. Pour the hot chocolate into the bottom of the mug. Pour the coffee over the back of a spoon so that the coffee sits on top of the hot chocolate. Gently spoon the cream on top and garnish with chocolate shavings.

WHITE HOT CHOCOLATE WITH LAVENDER

Beautifully indulgent with a slight hint of lavender, although you can leave out the lavender if you prefer to enjoy this as an unadulterated chocolate drink.

SERVES 2

Ingredients
250 ml (8½ oz) whole (full-fat) milk
250 ml (8½ oz) double (heavy) cream
½ teaspoon vanilla extract
225 g (8 oz) white chocolate chips
1 tablespoon dried lavender, plus extra to serve (optional)
whipped cream and marshmellows, to serve

Equipment
saucepan, wooden spoon, tea strainer, 2 mugs

Method
Warm the milk, cream, vanilla and chocolate chips in a saucepan over a low heat, stirring, until the milk is steaming and the chocolate has melted (do not let it boil). Stir in the lavender, if using, and take off the heat. Leave to infuse. Pour the hot chocolate through a strainer into the mugs. Serve with whipped cream, marshmallows and dried lavender.

CHILLI HOT CHOCOLATE

Add some spice to your night-time treat.

SERVES 3–4

Ingredients
800 ml (28 oz) whole milk
1 vanilla bean, split lengthways
1 long red chilli, split lengthways
½ tablespoon chilli flakes
2 cloves
1 cinnamon stick
170 g (6 oz) dark (bittersweet) chocolate chips
pinch of salt
whipped cream, to serve

Equipment
saucepan, wooden spoon, sieve, heatproof jug,
whisk, ladle, 3–4 mugs

Method
Simmer the milk, vanilla bean, chilli, chilli flakes,
cloves and cinnamon in a saucepan for 15 minutes,
stirring occasionally. Strain into a heatproof jug,
then pour back into the saucepan. Warm the milk
and add the chocolate and salt, whisking gently.
Ladle into mugs. Serve with whipped cream.

MULLED PEAR & APPLE

Spiced pears warmed up with cinnamon and apple
juice – a great alternative to anything else mulled!

SERVES 4

Ingredients
1 litre (34 oz) cloudy apple juice
2.5 cm (1 in) piece ginger, peeled and sliced
1 pear, cored and sliced
1 cinnamon stick, plus extra to garnish
2 cardamom pods
1 tablespoon light brown sugar
zest and juice of 2 limes

Equipment
saucepan, wooden spoon, ladle, 4 mugs

Method
Put all of the ingredients into a saucepan over
a medium heat and slowly bring up to the boil,
stirring occasionally. When all of the sugar has
dissolved, take the pan off the heat and ladle
into mugs. Serve with a stick of cinnamon in each
mug to garnish.

WARM DATE & CASHEW MILK

SERVES 2

A nutty milk like no other. This is slightly sweetened with dates rather than sugar, so it's lower on calories too!

❶ INGREDIENTS

500 ml (17 oz) unsweetened almond milk
3 dates, pitted
120 g (4 oz) cashew nuts

❷ EQUIPMENT

BLENDER   SAUCEPAN   2 MUGS   WOODEN
                                 SPOON

❸ METHOD

Blend all of the ingredients together until smooth. Pour the mixture into a saucepan and slowly bring up to a simmer over a low heat. Simmer for 5 minutes, stirring occasionally, then remove from the heat. Pour into mugs and serve.

SPICED APPLE

The ultimate hot appley drink with spices to give you comfort and pleasure.

❶ INGREDIENTS

1.4 litres (2½ pints) apple juice
zest of 1 lemon
10 cloves
5 cardamom pods
3 star anise
2 cinnamon sticks
1 cm (½ in) piece ginger, peeled
1 teaspoon light brown sugar (optional)
2 sweet apples, to garnish

❷ EQUIPMENT

SAUCEPAN   4–6 MUGS   HEATPROOF JUG OR BOWL   SIEVE   STAR COOKIE CUTTER

❸ METHOD

Put all the ingredients, except the apples, into a saucepan over a medium heat and bring to a simmer. Simmer for 10 minutes, then remove the pan from heat, cover and leave to steep for 1 hour. Place the pan back on the heat and warm through. Meanwhile, slice the apples crossways into thin circles and cut out star shapes using a cookie cutter, removing any pips from the centre of the stars. Strain the mixture into a heatproof jug or bowl, then ladle the hot punch into mugs and garnish with some apple stars.

FERN GREEN

Hot on juicing and constantly on the look-out for fab tasting non-alcoholic drinks, Fern Green is a food writer, stylist, and chef living in the UK and Italy. She has written a series of health cookbooks as well as *Breakfast: Morning, Noon and Night*. She loves to entertain, not only her guests in Italy, but also to her friends and family in the UK, thinking up delicious recipes and crafting out speciality drinks. Her current favourite mocktail is the seasonal spiced ginger and winter soda. She loves a drink with a kick.

ACKNOWLEDGEMENTS

A big juicy thank you to Kate Pollard, Kajal Mistry and all at Hardie Grant UK – you work so bloody hard, have a drink on me; the designer Jim Green (no relation!) and the incredible illustrator Esme Lonsdale…I'd love a poster in the same style on my wall; Malcolm for letting me take over your kitchen all afternoon testing; Lois, my lovely mum, for slurping up the shakes with such vigour; and Sue Green for giving my husband such a sweet tooth!

INDEX

COCONUT WATER

CUSTARD CREAM

The Mocktail Manual by Fern Green

First published in 2016 by Hardie Grant Books

Hardie Grant Books (UK)
5th & 6th Floor
52–54 Southwark Street
London, SE1 1UN
www.hardiegrant.co.uk

Hardie Grant Books (Australia)
Ground Floor, Building 1
658 Church Street
Melbourne, VIC 3121
www.hardiegrant.com.au

British Library Cataloguing-in-Publication Data.
A catalogue record for this book is available from the British Library.

ISBN 978-1-78488-021-7

Publisher: Kate Pollard
Senior Editor: Kajal Mistry
Cover and Internal Design: Jim Green
Illustrator: © Esme Lonsdale
Editors: Susan Pegg and Lorraine Jerram
Indexer: Cathy Heath
Colour Reproduction by p2d

Printed and bound in China by 1010

10 9 8 7 6 5 4 3 2 1